*Rosicrucians and
Speculative Masonry
in the
Seventeenth Century*

By Ossian Lang

Copyright © 2020 Lamp of Trismegistus. All rights reserved. No part of this publication may be reproduced or transmitted in any form or by any means, electronic or mechanical, including photocopying, recording, or by any information storage and retrieval system, without permission in writing from Lamp of Trismegistus. Reviewers may quote brief passages.

ISBN: 978-1-63118-489-5

*Foundations of Freemasonry
Series*

Other Books in this Series and Related Titles

Masonic and Rosicrucian History by M P Hall & H Voorhis (978-1-63118-486-4)

The Kabbalah of Masonry & Related Writings by E Levi &c (978-1-63118-453-6)

Some Deeper Aspects of Masonic Symbolism by A E Waite (978-1-63118-461-1)

Masonic Symbolism of King Solomon's Temple by A Mackey &c (978-1-63118-442-0)

The Old Past Master by Carl H Claudy (978-1-63118-464-2)

The Mysteries of Freemasonry & the Druids by various (978-1-63118-444-4)

Royal Arch, Capitular and Cryptic Masonry by various (978-1-63118-425-3)

The Two Great Pillars of Boaz and Jachin by A Mackey &c (978-1-63118-433-8)

The Regius Poem or Halliwell Manuscript by King Solomon (978-1-63118-447-5)

The Lost Keys of Freemasonry or The Secret of Hiram Abiff (978-1-63118-427-7)

Masonic Symbolism of the Apron & the Altar by various (978-1-63118-428-4)

Symbolism and Discourses on the Entered Apprentice, Fellowcraft and Master Mason Blue Lodge Degrees by various (978-1-63118-413-0)

The Legend of the Holy Grail and its Connection with Templars and Freemasons by A E Waite (978-1-63118-462-8)

Freemasonry in the Medieval or Middle Ages by various (978-1-63118-450-5)

American Indian Freemasonry by A C Parker (978-1-63118-460-4)

Ancient Mysteries and Secret Societies by M P Hall (978-1-63118-410-9)

The Ceremony of Initiation: Analysis & Commentary (978-1-63118-473-4)

Masonic Life of George Washington by Albert G Mackey (978-1-63118-457-4)

The Janeites, The Man Who Would Be King and Other Stories of Freemasonry by Rudyard Kipling (978-1-63118-480-2)

Audio Versions are also available on Audible, Amazon and Apple

Table of Contents

Introduction…7

Rosicrucians and Speculative Masonry in the Seventeenth Century

Masonic Beginnings…9

Hints Pointing to Rosicrucian Origins…13

Presumptions…17

Rosicrucians or Rosy Cross Alchemists…19

Derivations of Masonic Symbols…21

Fludd and Frisius…23

Central Tenets of the Brethren of the Rosy Cross…25

More Light From the "Summum Bonum"…33

Rosicrucian Brethren as Master Builders and Form of the Lodge…35

The Royal Art…37

Conclusions…41

Postscript…51

INTRODUCTION

From the beginning of Modern Freemasonry's birthdate of 1717, the intelligentsia of humanity have found refuge for safe reflection within the walls of the fraternity. Masonic writers have produced a nearly incalculable amount of written musings on a multitude of esoteric and philosophical subjects, as they relate to the ancient mysteries that Freemasonry currently storehouses. Sadly, most of it appears to have sat largely unread, as American Freemasonry in particular, continues to transform itself into something that bears little resemblance to what it was originally designed to be. The true essence of Freemasonry is not that of blind patriotism or a single-minded national religion but one of Universal Brotherhood and altruism, designed for the betterment not just of its members but of society as a whole. In particular, for those who are not members of the fraternity, as Freemasonry has always acted as a beacon, to help guide humanity through darker times, with the hopes that one day we will collectively reach a truly enlightened age.

It's not uncommon for new members joining the fraternity to find little education within the walls of many modern lodges, in spite of so much written material available to the membership. Many older members are not simply uneducated with regards to real Masonic history and symbology, not to mention the vast arena of related subjects, but they are disinterested in all of it, as well.

Lamp of Trismegistus is doing its part to help preserve humanity's Masonic history by making some of these classics available to those students who are seeking to unearth the knowledge of these ancient colossi. As such, Lamp of Trismegistus offers its readers highlights of Masonic study, culled from a variety of authors and viewpoints, with the hope bringing education back into the fraternity. So, be sure to check out other titles in our *Foundations of Freemasonry Series* as well as our *Theosophical Classics, Occult Fiction, Paranormal Research Series, Esoteric Classics, Supernatural Fiction, Studies in Buddhism* and our *Christian Apocrypha Series* as well as numerous other subjects; and, don't be afraid to let a little altruism into your own heart or even into your Lodge. You can also download the audio versions of many of these titles from Audible, Amazon or Apple, for learning on the go.

ROSICRUCIANS AND SPECULATIVE MASONRY IN THE SEVENTEENTH CENTURY

MASONIC BEGINNINGS

By Ossian Lang

The birthyear of the present Grand Lodge period of Freemasonry is securely fixed. Of the time of establishment, between 1717 and 1723, we have only a few more or less unimportant data and next to nothing as regards reliable information explaining the momentous developments which must have taken place before "The Constitutions," the Magna Charta of modern Freemasonry, could be formulated and issued in printed form.

The reasons for the lack of reliable historical material concerning the status and activity of the Fraternity, before 1723, are simple enough. History recording is an after-thought. It arises when some degree of greatness, or at least the promise of greatness, is achieved. That is why Israelitic History began with David and Solomon.[1] That is why English history began with Alfred the Great. That is why Masonic history began with the Grand Mastership of John, Duke of Montagu, whose connection with the Fraternity aroused widespread interest in Freemasonry.

The publication of the Constitutions, in 1723, became a

---

[1] See "Early Hebrew History" by that distinguished authority on Old Testament literature, our R.'. W.'. Brother, the Rev. John Punnett Peters, Rector of St. Michael's Church, New York.

direct challenge to historians, and now began the questioning as to antecedents which has been going on ever since. Before the Grand Mastership of Montagu, there was nothing in the existence of the Fraternity in any way suggesting that this was destined to attain importance, let alone greatness. Of the lodges who united to form the premier Grand Lodge, only one evidenced real vitality. One soon became extinct. Another had to be reconstituted in 1723. A third retained only thirteen members between 1721 and 1723. There appeared to be no inducement to record history.

A suggestive side-light is thrown on existing conditions by a note in the autobiography of Dr. William Stukeley, F. R. S. (1687-1765), reading as follows:

> "His curiosity led him to be initiated into the mysterys of Masonry, suspecting it to be the remains of the mysterys of the antients; when, with difficulty, a number sufficient were to be found in all London. After this, it became a public fashion, not only to spread over Brittain and Ireland, but all Europe."

Those of us who have experienced what it means to initiate candidates with barely enough brethren present to form a lodge, can sympathize with Brother Stukeley. The point of historical significance in his recital is that on January 6th, 1721, the date when he was "made a Freemason," it was only "with difficulty" that "a number sufficient was to be found in all London" to welcome him and two other distinguished Londoners into the Fraternity.

Another interesting item is the entry in Dr. Stukeley's diary, under date of December 27th, 1721, as follows:

"We met at the Fountain Tavern, Strand, and by the consent of the Grand Master present, Dr. Beal (D. G. M.) constituted a lodge there, where I was chose Master."

That throws light on many things. Taken together with other available stray bits of information, the entry suggests that "the verbal consent of the Grand Master, or his Deputy, was sufficient to authorize the formation of a lodge." We find, further, that the now required qualifications for elevation to the chair, were not known in 1721. Brother Stukeley had been a Mason for less than a year when he was "chose Master."

The presence of the Grand Master, John, Duke of Montagu, is worth noting. Dr. Stukeley and the Duke had both been elected Fellows of the Royal Society in 1717. Both belonged also to the "Gentlemen's Society" of Spaulding, a literary club, which counted among its members a number of men who won distinction in Freemasonry: Desaguliers, the Earl of Dalkeith, and Lord Coleraine, Grand Masters of the Grand Lodge of England, 1719, 1723, 1727; Joseph Ames, David Casley, Francis Drake (the latter serving as Grand Master of the Grand Lodge of All England, 1761-2); Martin Folkes, Sir Richard Manningham and Dr. Thomas Manningham; Sir Andrew Michael Ramsey, Knight of St. Lazarus, reputed founder of the Scottish Rite, became a member of this Society, in March, 1729.

The astonishing progress of Freemasonry, after the accession to the Grand Mastership of John, Duke of Montagu, may be readily understood when we take into account his zeal for the Fraternity and the eminent men who were glad to co-operate with him. The rapid rise to importance among the social organizations of the British metropolis may be regarded as the first real impetus to the study of the antecedents of the

Fraternity. Each new edition of the Constitutions revealed evidences of serious efforts to arrive at a satisfactory explanation of origins.

There was no doubt then, as there is no doubt now, that the Fraternity had at one time been connected in some way with the craft gild of Masons. It was equally clear that the lodges which formed the premier Grand Lodge had been made up of "Accepted" Freemasons enjoying at one time membership in the Masons' Company of London, but forming a distinct division within that Company and having no direct interest in operative Masonry. The "Laws, Forms and usages" which the Fraternity had in common with the "Craft and Fellowship of Masons," were plausibly accounted for as having been derived from former gild connections. The differences were not explained so easily. It is here where the difficulty arose. The problem was how to account for the "curious secret brotherhood" of Accepted Freemasons, which was regarded as the true parent of the Fraternity. It has remained an open problem to this day. The task I have set myself for the present discussion is to suggest a solution as far as arguments in support of it may be presented in public print.

HINTS POINTING TO ROSICRUCIAN ORIGINS

Gould to whose faithful labors we shall ever be indebted for the gathering together of a vast amount of valuable material relating to the development of our Fraternity, found that there is practical unanimity among serious historians to the effect that "Freemasonry, as it emerged from the crucible in 1723, was the product of many evolutionary changes, consummated for the most part in the six years during which the craft had been ruled by a central authority." We shall agree to this, with one rather important reservation: The changes that were wrought, between 1717 and 1723, did not spring from a desire to create something altogether new, but rather to restore what was believed to have been the true character of the Fraternity in the past; hence an earlier order was assumed and served as a model for the "many evolutionary changes." The attitude of the restorers may be gathered from the "Defence of Masonry" appended to the printed Constitutions of 1734, from which I quote for our present purpose this passage:

"The system as taught in the regular lodges, may have some redundancies or defects, occasion'd by the ignorance or indolence of the old members. And indeed, considering through what obscurity and darkness the Mystery has been deliver'd down; the many centuries it has survived; the many countries and languages, and sects and parties, it has run through, we are rather to wonder it ever arriv'd to the present age without more imperfection. In short, I am apt to think that Masonry (as it is now explain'd) has in some circumstances declined from its original purity! It has run along in muddy streams, and, as it were, underground. But notwithstanding the great rust it may have contracted * * * there is (if I judge right) much of the old fabrick still remaining; the essential *Pillars of the Building* may be discover'd through the rubbish, tho' the superstructure be over-run with moss and ivy, and the stones by length of time be disjointed."

The scholarly brother who wrote this, had in mind a very definite idea of the derivation of Freemasonry. His very language, the italicized words, and the reference to "the essential Pillars of the Building," suggest to those familiar with these things, a fairly clear explanation he had elaborated for himself, as we shall see further on.

In connection with the cited extract from the "Defence of Masonry," I desire to invite your attention to the consideration of a newspaper item appearing in the London Daily Journal of September 5th, 1730:[2]

"It must be confessed that there is a Society abroad from whom the English Free-Masons (asham'd of their true Origin) have copied a few Ceremonies, and take great Pains to persuade the World that they are derived from them and are the same with them. These are called Rosicrucians * * *

"On this Society have our Moderns endeavor'd to ingraft themselves, tho' they know nothing of their material Constitutions, and are acquainted only with some of their Signs of Probation and Entrance, inasmuch that 'tis but of late years (being better informed by some kind Rosicrucian) that they knew John the Evangelist to be their right Patron, having before kept for his Day that dedicated to John the Baptist."

---

[2] As quoted by Gould who had access to the original.

Here we have in convenient form a summary of comments given currency by a number of contemporaneous critics of the Fraternity, chiefly dissatisfied old brethren wedded to the belief that Freemasonry was wholly derived from operative Masonry. By intimating that "our Moderns" were trying to "ingraft themselves" on the Society of Rosicrucians, they reveal a significant fact which is verified, though in veiled terms, by our quotation from the "Defence of Masonry." Bearing in mind that this "Defence" was published with the implied official sanction of the Grand Lodge, we must assume that the learned brethren who directed the inner affairs of the Fraternity, were convinced that the substance of Freemasonry was in nowise derived from operative Masonry, but that the "Mystery" had come down through the ages by way of quite a different channel. Since the suggestion is offered that the "Rosicrucians" were regarded as the true forebears, it will be worth our while to examine this question more closely.[3]

---

[3] In Scotland, too, we find allusions to a connection between the Brethren of the Rosy Cross and Masonry; as for instance in a poem forming part of Adamson's "Muses Threnodie," published at Edinburgh, in 1638. There in singing the praises of the beauties of Perthshire, the poet says:
"For we be brethren of the Rosie Cross:
"We have the Mason word and second sight."

PRESUMPTIONS

We shall have to take for granted certain matters discussed in my paper on "Medieval Craft Gilds and Freemasonry," published in *The Builder*.

(1) The Constitutions, including "Laws, Forms and Usages," reveal former external connections of the forebears of the Fraternity with gilds of operative Masons.

(2) The "drooping" lodges which united, in 1717, to form the Grand Lodge of England were of an essentially convivial character, possessing certain "antient" ceremonies and modes of recognition and guarding "mysteries" of the origin and meaning of which the remnant of the earlier "secret brotherhood" were ignorant.

(3) The earlier London lodge or lodges of "Accepted" (Speculative) Masons had no continuous history, revealing its existence rather by sporadic revivals of "an old order."

(4) Degrees, symbolism and ritualistic peculiarities known as "Arts and Sciences," consisted of borrowings from several sources, the selection and elaboration being governed, in the first two decades of the Grand Lodge, by deliberate efforts of the organizers of the work to restore the "Original purity of the old fabrick."

(5) The spirit of Freemasonry is a growth from beginnings which may he traced with some degree of certainty to societies quite different from those which contributed Constitutions and suggestions for initiatory ceremonies.

ROSICRUCIANS OR ROSY CROSS ALCHEMISTS

Our present inquiry will deal largely with explanations of presumptions three, four and five, and more particularly with the so-called Rosicrucian origins of Freemasonry.

Extensive researches regarding Alchemists and their reputed successors in Rosicrucianism, covering a vast and largely unprofitable literature on the subject, have led me to formulate a few conclusions which I shall present more or less categorically. A fuller discussion would be too cruel a trial of the fraternal patience of the readers of *The Builder*.

We shall probably never know for a certainty whether there ever was an organized Fraternity of the Rosy Cross. We do know there were reputed and professed Rosicrucians, particularly in the sixteenth and seventeenth centuries, and there were also distinguished leaders of thought who stoutly defended the doctrines ascribed to the Fraternity and many reputable men who adopted the Rosicrucian symbolism, in an extensive array of books. There is furthermore abundant testimony to warrant the inference that there were in existence "invisible" or secret societies and lodges composed of men seeking honestly to give realization to the practice of the art or arts described in these books as characteristic of the mystic Brethren of the Rosy Cross. The absence of a recognized authoritative central body was in the course of events taken advantage of by impostors parading under the name of Rosicrucians who played upon the credulity of the public till the name sank into general disrepute.

The English and Scottish Rosicrucians who are the only

ones to be taken into account for our purpose, were Christian Theosophists. Like their brethren on the European continent, they made much of Cabala, following chiefly the Alexandrinian Philo. Neo-Platonism or Neo-Pythagorism, the Old Testament and Christian theology also engaged their attention. They devoted themselves with fervor to the study of chemistry, physics, music, astronomy and mathematics (particularly geometry). Mystic, allegorical interpretation of the Scriptures was a characteristic trait. Their supreme object, however, to which all studies were subordinated, was the promotion of the welfare of humanity.

These Rosicrucians were the lineal descendants of the theosophic portion of the Alchemists who are sometimes called Hermetic Philosophers.

DERIVATION OF MASONIC SYMBOLS

Bearing in mind that Hermetics and the Rosy Cross fraternity are fundamentally the same, though they differ in name and somewhat in allegorical interpretation, let me now quote for you a letter by Albert Pike, addressed to the historian Gould, which contains this interesting reference to Hermetic symbols to be found in Freemasonry:

"I have been for some time collecting the old Hermetic and Alchemical works in order to find out what Masonry came into possession of from them. I have ascertained with certainty that the square and compasses, the triangle, the oblong square, the three Grand Masters, the idea embodied in the substitute word, the Sun, Moon and Master of the Lodge, and others were included in the number.

"The symbols that I have spoken of as Hermetic may have been borrowed by Hermeticism, but all the same it had them, and I do not know where they were used, outside of Hermeticism, until they appeared in Masonry.

"I think that the Philosophers, becoming Free Masons, introduced into Masonry its symbolism."

My own investigations have verified Albert Pike's conclusions. In fact, I would greatly extend the list of symbols, adding to them symbols which are to be found among the true Brethren of the Rosy Cross, with this result:

Purely Rosy Cross Symbols:[4] Jacob's ladder; rough and perfect Ashlar; Sun, Moon, and Master of the Lodge; flaming

---

[4] Or Rosy Cross and Hermetic combined,-or Alchemist symbols.

star; three Grand Masters; three columns; two pillars; circle between parallel lines; point within a circle; sacred delta (triangle); oblong; three, five and seven steps.

Symbols which the Operative Gild and Brethren of the Rosy Cross had in common: Square; compasses; level; plumb; trowel; bee-hive; horn of plenty; hour glass; cassia.

Purely Masonic: Three windows; twenty-four-inch gauge; gavel; trestle board; tesselated border.

The first and second lists might have been extended. We hope to have given enough, however, to suggest the indebtedness of Freemasonry to the Rosy Cross.

The choice of two explanations is offered. One is that implied in the quotation we have given from the London Daily Journal in 1730, which would have us conclude that "the English Free-Masons (asham'd of their true origin)" imported Rosy Cross symbols and ceremonials into the system of the Fraternity. The other is founded on the quoted passage from the "Defence," which tells in so many words that Freemasonry had come down the ages through the Fraternity of the Rosy Cross, that much had been lost on the way which the Grand Lodge of England sought to restore in its proper place. In other words, following the former allegation, the Grand Lodge adopted the Brethren of the Rosy Cross as forefathers; following the latter declaration, the Brethren of the Rosy Cross were the true forebears.

There is no reason for assuming that the Alchemists were the originators of the symbols referred to in the foregoing list. In fact, I am sure these symbols were borrowed from an older source.

FLUDD AND FRISIUS

We agreed to confine our attention chiefly to the theosophic Alchemists of England and Scotland. Let us limit the range still further by disregarding the older Alchemists and taking note only of the representative leaders of the later (if not the last) of the "True Brethren of the Rosy Cross."[5] Here we have an abundance of first hand information in the several treatises in defense of the mystic Fraternity by that renowned English physician and philosopher, Robert Fludd, and in the "Summum Bonum" (The Supreme Good), a Latin dissertation by a Scottish friend of Fludd's, who wrote under the pseudonym of Joachimus Frisius (or Frizius).

The Century Dictionary gives this brief biographical notice of Robert Fludd, or Flud: "Born at Bearsted, Kent, 1574, died at London, Sept. 8th, 1637. An English physician and mystical philosopher. He wrote several treatises in defense of the fraternity of the 'Rosy Cross." Waite, who presents a more extensive biography in "The Real History of the Rosicrucians," adds this word of appreciation: "The central figure of Rosicrucian literature * * * is Robertus de Fluctibus, the great English mystical philosopher of the seventeenth century, a man of immense erudition, of exalted mind, and, to judge by his writings, of extreme personal sanctity." Fludd was one of the last, if not the last, of the giants of universal scholarship of whom there were many, before the days of specialization set in. He was a devout Christian and a staunch Protestant, basing his philosophy of the universe frankly on the Bible.

---

[5] We exclude, of course, altogether the spurious Rosicrucianism which brought the name of the, Fraternity into disrepute by its grandiloquence and diletantism and the charlatanry and deliberate fraud carried on under its banner.

Of Joachimus Frisius, Frizius or Frize, whom we shall call Frisius, we know nothing, except that Fludd tells us he was a Scotchman and wrote his book partly in Scottish and partly in Latin. Fludd translated the Scottish portions into Latin, made a few slight changes in the text, and had the whole put into print, under the title of "Summum Bonum."

CENTRAL TENETS OF THE BRETHREN OF THE ROSY CROSS

Fludd and Frisius agree in essential points. As the "Summum Bonum" supplies all we need for our present purpose, we may gather from this work whatever information is desired for our inquiry. The central symbolism turns around the stone, Aben,[6] and the building of the House of Wisdom. There is an abundance of allegorical uses of the word stone or stones, in the Old and New Testaments, which are made use of by Frisius to justify the philosophy of the Brethren of the Rosy Cross.

ROBERT FLUDD

---

[6] Aben or Eben (as in Ebenezar) is Hebrew for stone.

"Thus saith the Lord of hosts: Consider your ways Go up to the hill-country and bring wood and build the house." --Haggai I, 78.

"They that are far off shall come and build in the temple of the Lord." --Zechariah VI, 15.

"Wisdom hath builded a house, She hath hewn out her seven pillars." --Proverbs IX, 1.

"Through wisdom is a house builded, "And by understanding it is established; "And by knowledge are the chambers filled "With all precious and pleasant riches." --Proverbs XXIV, 3-4.

"The wise man buildeth his house upon a rock. The rains may descend and the floods come; the winds may blow and beat upon that house: it will not fall; for it is founded upon a rock." --St. Matthew VII, 24-25.

Aben, Frisius argues, is the cabalistic stone. In it, we have the Holy Trinity. For in Hebrew, Ab means Father and Ben Son; but where the Father and the Son are present there the Holy Ghost must also be.

Aben is then explained as the foundation stone of the universe, the macrocosm. ("The Lord answered Job out of the whirlwind and said, Where wast thou when I laid the foundations of the earth? Declare if thou hast understanding. Whereupon are the foundations thereof fastened? or who laid the cornerstone thereof?"--Job XXXVIII, 1, 4, 6.)

The macrocosmic Aben, then, is the foundation stone of all and for all. It was laid in Zion, and all the prophets and apostles built upon it, though the ignorant and wicked builders rejected it as a stumbling block and stone of contention:

"Thus saith the Lord God: "Behold, I lay in Zion for a foundation a stone, "A tried stone, a costly corner-stone of sure foundation. "He that believeth shall not make haste. "And I will make justice the line, "And righteousness the plummet." --Isaiah XXVIII, 16-17.

"According to the grace of God which is given unto me as a wise Master builder, I have laid the foundation, and another buildeth thereon. But let every man take heed how he buildeth thereupon.... For other foundation can no man lay than that is laid, which is Jesus Christ." --St. Paul, 1; Cor. III, 10-11.

"The stone which the builders rejected "Is become the chief corner-stone." --Psalm CXVIII, 22.

"As it is written in the scripture, Behold, I lay in Zion a chief corner stone, elect, precious: and he that believeth in him shall not be confounded.

"Unto you, therefore, which believe, he is precious: but unto them which be disobedient, the stone which the builders disallowed, the same is made the head of the corner, and a stone of stumbling, and a rock of offence, even to them which stumble at the word, being disobedient." --I Peter II, 6-7-8.

If we consider the significance of Aben for the individual man (the microcosm, or the universe on a small scale), we find we are parts of the same spiritual stone, "cut out of that catholic (universal) rock":

"Coming to Christ, as unto a living stone, disallowed indeed of men, but chosen of God and precious: Ye also, as living stones, be ye built up a spiritual house." --I Peter II, 4-6.

In other words: Build yourselves upon Christ, as the foundation stone, as living stones, to a house of God.

"We are labourers together with God: Ye are God's husbandry, Ye are God's building." --I Cor. III, 9.

"Know ye not that ye are the temple of God, and that the Spirit of God dwelleth in you? If any man defile this temple of God, him shall God destroy; for the temple of God is holy which temple ye are." --I Cor. III, 16-17.

Nor are those excluded who are-not of our faith. The temple of God is built up of all men who seek Him and strive to know Him. Quoting John, the Baptist: "Say not within yourselves, 'We have Abraham for our father': for I say unto you, That God is able of these stones to raise up children unto Abraham."

The plan of the building which the Fraternity of the Rosy Cross is seeking to establish is given in the words of Hebrews XIII, 1: "Let brotherly love continue."

"Behold, how good and how pleasant it is for brethren to dwell together in unity." --Psalm CXXXIII, 1.

An example of the mystic, allegorical interpretation of the Scriptures, met with everywhere in Rosy Cross literature, is the following:

As Christ was hidden in that Rock or Stone, before the days

of Moses, since the spiritual is usually concealed in the physical, so also does Moses conceal in his writings the spiritual Aben; that is why we say he wrote under a veil, i. e. mystically. That is why the Apostle Paul says (II Cor. III, 6) "The letter killeth, but the spirit giveth life."

"The Lord said unto Moses, Behold, I will stand before thee, there upon the rock in Horeb; and thou shall smite the rock, and there shall come water out of it, that the people may drink." --Exodus XVII, 6.

"Moreover, brethren, I would not that ye should be ignorant, how that all our fathers were under the cloud, and all passed through the sea; "And were all baptized unto Moses in the cloud and in the sea; "And did all eat the same spiritual meal; "And did all drink the same spiritual drink; for they drank of that spiritual Rock that went with them: and that Rock was Christ." --I Cor. X, 1-4.

Alchemistically expressed, the water which sprang from the Rock was potable gold, the word of God, words of Wisdom.

That suggests also what we Alchemists mean when we speak of producing gold. It is not the gold the multitude hankers for. Ours is living gold, the gold of God, that which the Psalmist calls silver:

"The words of the Lord are pure words, "As silver tried in a crucible on the earth, refined seven times." --Psalm XII, 7.

The Rosy Cross alchemy in the transmutation of base metals into gold, is not that of the spurious Rosicrucians who deceive the avaricious by false promises; it takes the base, natural man and turns him by its art into a new, spiritual man, through the Word of God and the practice of charity.

In the same manner the rough ashlar is turned into a perfect ashlar.

As God has promised to dwell among men, to have his tabernacle among them, we must with all our strength and with spiritual tools strive for Aben. As the prophet Isaiah says: "Ye that seek the Lord, Look unto the rock whence ye were hewn." (Isaiah LI, 1.)

The first step toward finding this Rock (the Philosopher's Stone) is to look for it within yourself; hence begin to know thyself. If you desire help from the writings of the Alchemists, remember that these wrote them in a veiled, mystic manner. Thus Darnaeus says "Change--oh! change yourselves from dead stones into living philosophical stones !"

In order to realize the chemical steps of progression, we must first seek to discover the true sense of the Alchemists through careful insight. Then it will be found that they wrote differently and wanted to be understood differently. (Masonically speaking, one must first possess "the key of a fellowcraft" to interpret correctly.)

We summarize, as follows; always following the "Summum Bonum":

The human body is a temple. Christ is its cornerstone. When we raise this corner-stone, His temple is also raised, as was the Temple of Solomon, when his players were fulfilled and the glory of the Lord descended.

"Similarly, Kephas and Aben were at one time only dead stones, now become living stones through an actual transmutation, in that from the condition of Adam after his fall from grace they transformed themselves into Adam's original state of innocence and perfection; just as if there had been effected a transmutation from ordinary dirty lead into the purest gold. And this transmutation took place by the intermediation of that living gold as of the mystic stone of the Philosophers, which to us represents the divine emanation of wisdom. This wisdom, however, is the gift of God, and nothing else."

MORE LIGHT FROM THE "SUMMUM BONUM"

The study of true Magic, the Cabala and chemistry are the sciences called the three principal columns of the house of wisdom. By Magic is meant the art of wisdom practiced by the Magi who came to worship the new born Christ. Cabala stands for mystic mathematics (or strength). Chemistry is explained as the study of nature (beauty). The true Brethren of the Rosy Cross are called architects who build the house of God, after the manner already explained.

Why did the Brethren adopt the name of the Rosy Cross? There is an order of the Holy Cross. The Knights who went to war against the Saracens bore on their cloaks the emblem of a deep red cross. The Brethren have chosen the true and living cross of Christ as the emblem of wisdom, that mystic wisdom which the Bible calls the Tree of Life whose root is the Word of Light.

The color of the cross is that of blood or as that of red roses mixed with lilies.

(We omit all mystic elaboration of the ideas here briefly indicated nor do we include other matters which have no bearing on the development of the Freemasonry of the Symbolic Lodge.)

ROSICRUCIAN BRETHREN AS MASTER BUILDERS AND FORM OF THE LODGE

Finally, the Brother is to labor at the perfecting of this work in the character of an architect, or master builder. (I Cor. III, 10-11).

In order that the structure may be firmly established, in order that we may arrive at the rosy blood of the cross hidden within the foundation stone, we must dig from the surface to the center, we must seek and knock; unless we pursue our work with zeal, all our efforts will be wasted. All bodies have manifest height, occult depth and intermediate breadth. From the manifest form of a body we can only conjecture what its occult form must be, when we destroy the manifest to advance to the revelation of its occult form. The truth of this is found when we contemplate the depth of the geometric cube.

The wise artist and the true religious philosopher must penetrate the earth and labor in every particle of the threefold dimension, if he wants to find the true rectangular foundation stone which God has laid in the foundation of the earth (Job 38, 4-6). Then he will know that "the love of Christ passeth knowledge, and that ye might be filled with all the fullness of God." (Eph. III, 19).

Then knock and strike zealously and strenuously, for "Ye have not yet resisted unto blood, striving against sin." (Heb. XII, 4). Here the Apostle teaches us occultly that a transgression here, something foreign there, not emanating from the pure truth which is Christ Jesus, is present, which must be broken off and gotten rid of, from the human or soul-endowed stone; then truth will illumine the master builder and true Brother, and it will gleam in a rose-red or blood-colored glow, and he will see in this divine light his own light and receive and enjoy at last the wages of his labors. Then he shall be justly called a Brother of the Rosy Cross and he shall be called a member of the true Fraternity.

THE ROYAL ART

Everything thus far has been gathered from the "Summum Bonum," arranged so as to serve best our present purpose and in language more suitable to our times, without however changing the essence and the spirit. I shall add no extended comment. The brethren who are at home in the language, the symbols and the spirit of Freemasonry can gather their own conclusions. What has been gleaned from the work of Frisius, together with the notes on the symbolism of the Alchemists, would seem to be quite sufficient to explain why the Brethren of the Rosy Cross should have been considered the forebears of the Accepted Free Masons. Before offering a brief concluding summary, we must give a moment's attention to the development of the idea of the Royal Art which is the true name of Freemasonry.

First let us take another word from the "Summum Bonum," which describes the Rosy Cross view of the Royal Art:

There were in antiquity, four renowned schools of natural Magic, to-wit, the Hindoo, the Persian, the Chaldaic and the Egyptian. From the Persians came those three Kings (Magi, Wise Men) who were seeking the new born "King of the Jews," to present gifts unto Him and to worship Him. The sons of Persian Kings, as Plato has related in his "Alcibiades," were initiated into Magic that they might learn from the study of the pattern of the universe how best to govern their own dominions and to preserve order and administer justice therein. Cicero, too, speaks of this, in his "De Divinatione," saying that no one was crowned among the Persians with the royal diadem until after he had been fully instructed in Magic. That is why Oriental kings were so well grounded in wisdom and coveted the name of Magi or Wise Men. Hence those who came from the far East to worship the Christ child, were called by the Holy Spirit "Magi."

Recalling that in the early days of the Grand Lodge of England we met repeatedly with the declaration, "There have been Kings that have been of this sodality," we shall have another clue to the genealogy of Freemasonry, as it was conceived by the organizers of the speculative craft.

Or take this quotation from "The Master's Song" of the premier Grand Lodge:

Thus mighty Eastern Kings, and some Of Abram's Race, and Monarchs good Of Egypt, Syria, Greece and Rome. True Architecture understood.

Who can unfold the ROYAL Art? Or sing its Secrets in a Song? They're safely kept in Mason's heart And to the ancient Lodge belong.

Those familiar with the Constitutions of 1723 know what changes were made to make the ancient "Charges" conform to the newly established ideals of the Fraternity. What was there said regarding the attitude toward the "old Gothic Constitutions," applies also to the religious tenets of the Brethren of the Rosy Cross. The changes gave a simplified definition of the "Royal Art," though the spirit remained what it had been in the "Summum Bonum." Indicating the new meaning in the briefest form, I would answer:

What is the Royal Art? The practice of the Royal Law. And the Royal Law?

"If ye fulfill the Royal Law according to the Scripture, Thou shalt love thy neighbor as thyself, ye do well." So wrote St. James, the first Bishop of Jerusalem, the same who declared that "Pure religion and undefiled before God and the Father is this; to visit the fatherless and widows in their affliction, and to keep himself unspotted from the world."

CONCLUSIONS

In conclusion, I beg to submit a summary statement embodying findings based on many years of search to arrive at some sort of satisfactory solution of the puzzling question as to the derivation of the substance of Freemasonry. This summary is not complete and is intended to serve merely as a supplement to my paper on "Freemasonry and the Medieval Craft Gilds."

The establishment of Christianity was accomplished chiefly by the marvelous rise of the power of the Church and the rigid application of this power. The first need and therefore the first care was to establish catholic unity in the faith.

The disintegration of that which had been the Roman Empire had sounded the death knell for pagan civilization. An era of confusion followed. The most extravagant teachings were in circulation. Passions and vices ran riot because of the prevailing anarchy. A cult of a thousand years had been dispossessed by a young cult which had the promise of eternity but had not then been established firmly enough to compel respect. People hesitated between the creed of the yesterday and the creed of the tomorrow. There was one giant among men, who had the courage to choose, and having chosen, to battle for his creed without weakening. That was St. Augustin, the great Doctor of the Church, mystic and man of action, philosopher and master organizer and administrator. He united in himself the genius of the Semitic race with the wisdom of the Latins, the Greeks and the Alexandrians. He may well be called the establisher of the Roman Church which became, and for a thousand years thereafter remained, the supreme ruler of

Western Europe.[7]

One indirect but quite logical effect of St. Augustin's war upon heresies was the suppression of every form of free speculation in philosophy. Unity of creed must be established at any cost. The apostasy of the Emperor Julian had convinced doubting ecclesiastics of the danger lurking in an unbridled freedom of study. Three years after the death of St. Augustin, the Fourth Council of Carthage (in 398) formally prohibited the reading of secular books even by the bishops. In 529, the philosophical schools were abolished by decree of Emperor Julian.[8]

Freedom of thought cannot be suppressed by decrees. But a check may be put on the expression of thought. And it was put on. Then there sprang up secret ("invisible") Colleges, Academies, Lodges, etc., for meetings of independent seekers after truth. In Italy, particularly, these secret associationsdisplayed great activity, hiding their real purposes under names, auspices and forms selected to mislead the watchful spies of the hierarchy.[9]

Members of the Academy of the Trowel, for example, would wear builders' aprons and display builders' tools, presenting the appearance of a gild of operative Masons. By giving mystic meanings to emblems of a seemingly operative character, they could freely discuss prohibited topics in a manner only understood by trusted initiates. If they wished to be regarded as men engaged in architectural subjects, they would try to have those present who were generally reputed to

---

[7] For a vivid picture of life in the fourth century, the period so trying for men's souls, I refer those who read French to the charming, wonderful book of Louis Bertrand on "St. Augustin."

[8] See Laurie's "Rise of Universities," first two chapters.

[9] Especially from the fourteenth century onward.

be interested in such matters. The membership was made up largely of scientists, philosophers, architects, musicians, painters, sculptors and poets.

In spite of their camouflage, the brethren of these "invisible" lodges were occasionally discovered. Yet so well were their secrets guarded that practically no first hand knowledge of them has come down to us, though we can obtain information enough from Roman Catholic sources, if we make proper allowances for always unmistakable prejudices. Thus Pastor in his famous "History of the Popes" refers to the "invisible" Roman Academy founded by Julius Pomponius Laetus, professor in the University of Rome, in the fifteenth century, as "the center of meetings for all discontented and pagan Humanists." We are told that the initiates adopted religious usages, regarded themselves as a college of priests, with Pomponius as Grand High Priest. Gregovorius who is quoted with approval, calls the Academy "a classical Freemasons Lodge."

The Brethren of the Academy of Pomponius were accused, under Pope Paul II (1464-1471), as having conspired to kill the Holy Father, that they were pagans and materialists, etc. Imprisonment and death threatened the Brethren. "Safety first" in those days meant punishing the accused first and investigating afterward. Most of the Academicians fled. Ultimately all were, on the principle of Scotch verdict, absolved from the charge of heresy. Owing to the intervention of the scholarly and liberal Cardinal Bessarion, Pomponius and the others were allowed the freedom of the city, under close surveillance.

The Academicians were predominantly Platonists. So were the members of most of the other forbidden secret societies (or occasional gatherings), while the Church officially upheld Aristotle and for a long time sought to suppress Plato to whom religion consisted essentially in the practice of justice.

In the Teutonic countries, speculative philosophers were to be found largely among the mystic Alchemists who are often spoken of as "Hermetic Philosophers," in Masonic writings. They had no central organization. Wherever two or three of them met together, they formed a lodge for mutual intercourse and the initiation of worthy candidates who, after a period of probation more or less extended, would be put in possession of the secret symbols and traditions whereby they might obtain a key to the literature of all the mystics.

In Great Britain, the Rosicrucian Alchemists were, as has been indicated, essentially Christian theosophists. They studied nature, but not for purely scientific purposes; they sought rather to discover in nature the traces of the mystic Supreme Architect of the Universe, revealed as well as concealed in and by the visible and discoverable phenomena.

The predominance of religious speculation led to the separation from the mystic Alchemists of those who preferred to specialize in the experimental study of nature. The philosophical reform work of Francis Bacon (1561-1626) was probably the chief cause of the change.

At the beginning of the seventeenth century, through the influence of Robert Fludd (1574-1671), the Fraternity of the Rosy Cross arose in Great Britain. This Fraternity represented the mystic portion of the Alchemists whose practices they followed. "Heresy" had been no safer under the Protestant "Bloody Bess" than it had been in Pre-Reformation times; the only difference being in the kind of "heresy" for which men were hanged or burned by the executioner of the power which happened to be in control at the time. That, together with the predilection for symbols having to do with house and temple building, no doubt accounts for the appearance of the names of reputed Rosicrucianism the membership lists of the operative gild of Masons. The Alchemists of an earlier day are supposed also to have been identified with this particular gild. The inference is that they formed occasional lodges of their own and were the "secret brotherhood" in the bosom of the Masons Company referred to in the records of that Company. This would account for the presence among the "Accepted" Masons of Elias Ashmole, Sir Robert Moray, Dr. Thomas Wharton, Sir George Wharton, William Oughtred, Dr. John Hewitt, the astronomer and astrologist, William Lily and Sir Christopher Wren, all of them distinguished scientists interested in the Rosy Cross program.

And now a word to account for the statement in the Constitutions of 1738, at a time when there were many alive who would have objected to it if it had not been true, that the decay of the lodges of Accepted Freemasons, shortly after 1708, was due to Sir Christopher Wren's neglect of the office of Grand Master. Gould's insistence that Wren was not a Freemason and never could have been Grand Master, in spite of trustworthy evidence which should have caused him not to be so positive, is easily explained. Gould is usually very careful, content with nothing but the original sources but it is quite evident here that he had never given serious consideration to the possibility of Rosy Cross relationships.

Sir Christopher Wren was a speculative Mason, nevertheless, and may have been known as Grand Master of the "Accepted" circle. His "neglect of the office" shortly after 1708 appears quite natural to me. That which had attracted him into the "Acceptation" was no doubt the caliber of the men who were associated with it and who were active in it. But, in 1662, there had been incorporated in London the Royal Society, which as time went on, absorbed more and more the spare time of the men more directly interested in scientific progress. After the close of the seventeenth century, "acceptation" of men of this stamp in the Masonic fraternity ceased altogether. The lodges became mere convivial clubs and for these Sir Christopher had no time.

This leads me to advance a conclusion for which I hope to have prepared the ground. I believe that the Royal Society and Freemasonry both sprang from the same original source or sources.

"Alchemy" which comprised in Pre-Reformation days all pursuits in science and philosophy had passed into Rosicrucianism. Bacon's "Novum Organum," in 1620, having established the necessity for specialization in experimental science, Rosicrucianism was doomed to final extinction. Bacon's "New Atlantis" (1624) set up a new ideal for men eager to enlist in the service of mankind by the advancement of civilization.[10]

"The New Atlantis" was written, as Diderot pointed out in the prospectus of the French Encyclopedistes, "at a time when, so to say, neither sciences nor arts existed." The twilight efforts of the Alchemists no longer sufficed. More light was wanted. Day was at hand. "Solomon's House, that beautiful dream of the philosopher, began to be realized less than forty years after

---

[10] "Doubtless it was one of Bacon's highest hopes that from the growth of true knowledge would follow in surprising ways the relief of man's estate; this, as an end, runs through all his yearning after a fuller and surer method of interpreting nature." --Dean Church.

his death."[11] The picture of Solomon's House drawn by Bacon in "The New Atlantis" was the model from which the Royal

DECPICTION OF BACON'S NEW ATLANTIS

---

[11] M.C. Adam's "Philosophie de F. Bacon," Paris, 1890, p. 328. Bacon died on April 9th, 1626. The London "College of Philosophy" which became the Royal Society, was instituted in 1645.

Society was built.[12] The historian of this Society, Dr. Thomas Sprat (1636-1713) Bishop of Rochester, made acknowledgment of this when he wrote: "I shall only mention one great man who had the true imagination of the whole extent of this enterprise, as it is now set on foot, and that is Lord Bacon."[13]

Professor Nichol sums up the established testimony of all authorities on the subject, in these words:[14] "It is admitted that the suggestion of the College of Philosophy instituted in London (1645) and after the Restoration extended into the Royal Society (1662) was due to the prophetic scheme of Solomon's House in the New Atlantis. Wallis, one of the founders of the Society, exalts him by name, along with Galileo, as heir master. Sprat says "It was a work becoming the largeness of Bacon's wit to devise and the greatness of Clarendon's prudence to establish." Boyle invokes for its inauguration "that profound naturalist * * * one great Verulam."

The spirit that animated the whole conception of Solomon's House was "the love of man and the honoring of God." The Royal Society limited its membership quite naturally to men considered capable of rendering eminent service to the advancement of scientific discovery. Thereby it assured the progress of the great work it had undertaken, but it limited, at the same time, the realization of the ideal pictured in the "New Atlantis." The consciousness of this fact, together with the remembrances of the derivation from the true seekers after truth among the earlier Alchemists, were, I am persuaded, the chief reasons which prompted many of the members of the Royal Society to join the "revived" Society of Freemasons,

---

[12] G.C. Moorr Smith, in his edition of "The New Atlantis,' (Pitt Press Series) Cambridge, 1900, page 28.

[13] "History of the Royal Society," edition of 1667, page 35.

[14] "Francis Bacon; His life and Philosophy," (Blackwood's Phil. Classics) 1889, vol. II, p. 136.

shortly after the establishment of the Grand Lodge of England. In Freemasonry they hoped for the complete and universal realization of the whole ideal of the "New Atlantis," with the Royal Society as the scientific center of Solomon's House.

This is, briefly and summarily told, my conclusion regarding the evolution of "Speculative" Freemasonry, more particularly during the seventeenth century, for "the love of man and the honoring of God." Imperfectly as the result of my researches is placed before you, my brethren, I hope to have at least suggested where to look for traces of the origins of our beloved Fraternity founded upon the Fatherhood of God, the mystic foundation stone of the universe, and the practice of the Royal Art which is the fulfilment of the Royal Law according to the Scripture: "Thou shalt love thy neighbor as thyself.'

POSTSCRIPT

I trust I have not given the impression that the substance of modern Freemasonry was derived from the Rosicrucians. An organized Fraternity of the Rosy Cross probably never existed outside of books. The writings of Fludd and Frisius formulated for Great Britain a body of Rosy Cross tenets differing in essential points from the teachings of the Rosicrucians of Continental Europe. English and Scottish Alchemists followed Fludd and Frisius. Their attempts to translate the plans of these leaders into practice, appears to have induced some of them to form occasional lodges, either independently under the designation of Freemasons--the name of Rosicrucian having fallen into disrepute--or in the bosom of Masonic craft gilds, as a separate "secret brotherhood" of Accepted Freemasons. Read in connection with "Freemasonry and the Medieval Craft Gilds," the suggestion will be clearly understood.

Freemasonry, as established by the Constitutions of 1722-1723, represents the confluence of two streams, each having many tributaries: The sources of the one stream must be looked for in the Anglo-Saxon guild, and its name is democracy; the sources of the other must be looked for in the earliest academies of philosophers searching for the One Living God, Father of all men, and its name is liberty of conscience.

www.ingramcontent.com/pod-product-compliance
Lightning Source LLC
LaVergne TN
LVHW041501070426
835507LV00009B/728